GW01385445

On Holiday
En Vacances

French with

Max et Mathilde ™

Published by Blue Giraffe Press

inquiries@bluegiraffepress.com

www.bluegiraffepress.com

Blue Giraffe Press Ltd. Registered office: Richmond, England

Text and illustrations © Blue Giraffe Press Ltd 2007

Illustrated by Daryl Stevenson. Written by language consultant Carol Ellison

A catalogue record for this book is available from The British Library

All rights reserved

Colour reproduction by Vivid • UK • www.vividprepress.com

Printed in China

Je m'appelle
My name is

_____

A few tips for grown-ups!

The book and CD can be used on different levels. The left-hand page introduces the child to a single word. This word is then included in a simple sentence. Stick to this if that's what you feel is most appropriate.

On the right-hand page, the dialogue delivered by Max et Mathilde introduces a slightly higher level of vocabulary and expression.

Let the pictures guide the child. A translation appears at the back of the book rather than on the page itself to avoid word-for-word translation.

Pronunciation is modelled by Max et Mathilde on the audio CD. Repetition and singing along will reinforce the vocabulary and phrases in the book.

The most important thing is to maintain the child's enthusiasm, motivation and interest in learning French. Above all, keep it simple and fun!

la valise

Max et Mathilde partent
en vacances.
Ils font leurs valises.

la voiture

Ils partent en voiture.
Tout le monde est prêt.

« Vite Noisette !

« Tu pars aussi en vacances avec nous ! »

l'hôtel

Max et Mathilde arrivent à l'hôtel.
Ils ont chaud. Ils veulent aller à la
plage tout de suite.

"Dépêche-toi, Max!"

"Mais où est mon maillot de bain?"

9

la mer

L'hôtel est à côté de la mer.
Les enfants font du kayak.

"Je vais plus vite que toi Max!"

"Mais je te rattrape."

la plage

Les enfants adorent la plage.
Ils font des pâtés de sable.

"Fais attention, Noisette!"

le restaurant

Chaque soir Max et Mathilde
dînent au restaurant
avec maman et papa.

la glace

C'est le dernier jour des vacances.
Les enfants prennent une glace
avant de partir.

Translation

3

"Bonjour!" *"Hello!"*
Viens en vacances avec nous! *Come on holiday with us!*
Nous allons au bord de la mer. *We're going to the seaside.*
"Tu vas t'amuser! *You'll have fun"*
"Je m'appelle Max." *"I'm called Max."*
"Je m'appelle Mathilde." *"I'm called Mathilde."*
"Notre chien s'appelle Noisette!" *"Our dog's called Noisette."*

4-5

la valise *the suitcase*
Max et Mathilde partent en vacances. *Max et Mathilde are going on holiday.*
Ils font leurs valises. *They're packing their suitcases.*
"Youpii... c'est enfin les vacances." *"Hurrah...The holidays are here at last!"*
"Maman, ma valise est trop petite. *"Mum, my suitcase is too little.*
"Elle ne ferme pas!" *"It won't close!"*

6-7

la voiture *the car*
Ils partent en voiture. *They're going by car.*
Tout le monde est prêt. *Everyone's ready.*
"Vite, Noisette. Tu pars aussi en vacances avec nous!"
"Quick, Noisette. You're coming on holiday with us too!"

8-9

l'hôtel *the hotel*
Max et Mathilde arrivent à l'hôtel. *Max et Mathilde arrive at the hotel.*
Ils ont chaud. *They're hot.*
Ils veulent aller à la plage tout de suite. *They want to go straight to the beach*
"Dépêche-toi, Max!" *"Hurry up, Max!"*
"Mais où est mon maillot de bain?" *"But where are my swimming trunks?"*

10-11

la mer *the sea*
L'hôtel est à côté de la mer. *The hotel is by the sea.*
Les enfants font du kayak. *The children are kayaking.*
"Je vais plus vite que toi Max!" *"I'm going faster than you Max!"*
"Mais je te rattrape." *"But I'm catching up with you."*

12-13

la plage *the beach*
Les enfants adorent la plage. *The children love the beach.*
Ils font des pâtés de sable. *They are making sand-castles.*
"Fais attention, Noisette!" *"Be careful, Noisette!"*

14-15

le restaurant *the restaurant*
Chaque soir Max et Mathilde dînent au restaurant avec maman et papa.
Every evening Max et Mathilde eat supper in a restaurant with mum and dad.
"Que désirez-vous?" *"What would you like?"*
"Une pizza, s'il vous plaît Monsieur." *"A pizza, please!"*

16-17

la glace *the ice-cream*
C'est le dernier jour des vacances. *It's the last day of the holidays.*
Les enfants prennent une glace avant de partir. *The children are having an ice-cream before leaving.*
"Au revoir! A l'année prochaine." *"Bye-bye. See you next year."*

Max et Mathilde's Holiday Phrases

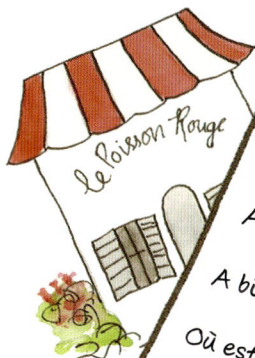

Bonjour! Hello!

Bonsoir! Good evening!

Au revoir! Goodbye!

A bientôt! See you soon!

Où est...? Where is...?

Où est la plage? Where is the beach?

Où est l'hôtel? Where is the hotel?

Où est le restaurant? Where is the restaurant?

Où est la piscine? Where is the swimming pool?

Allons à la plage. Let's go to the beach.

Allons au restaurant. Let's go to the restaurant.

J'ai faim. I'm hungry.

J'ai soif. I'm thirsty.

Je voudrais...I would like...

Je voudrais une glace à la vanille. I'd like a vanilla ice-cream

Je voudrais une glace au chocolat. I'd like a chocolate ice-cream

Je voudrais un coca. I'd like a coca-cola.

Je voudrais une pizza. I'd like a pizza.

J'adore nager. I love swimming.

Moi aussi! Me too!

Rentrons... Let's go back...

Rentrons à l'hôtel. Let's go back to the hotel.

le Poisson Rouge

Hôtel de la Plage

Now listen to us on the CD.
We'll say everything in French and English, and then you can
try repeating. Afterwards we can sing the holiday song together!

Max et Mathilde's Holiday Song

Nous partons pour les vacances!
Nous allons nous amuser.
Nous allons manger des glaces
Montons vite dans la voiture!

Les vacances en plein soleil,
Les vacances en plein soleil!

Nous n'allons plus à l'école,
Nous allons nous amuser.
Nous partons pour les vacances!
Montons vite dans la voiture!

Les vacances en plein soleil,
Les vacances en plein soleil!

We're going off on holiday!
We're going to have fun.
We're going to eat ice creams
Quick get in the car!

Holidays in the sunshine,
Holidays in the sunshine!

We're not going to school any more,
We're going to have fun.
We're going off on holiday!
Quick get in the car!

Holidays in the sunshine,
Holidays in the sunshine!